# The Dark Side of Condominiums and Other Life Experiences

George S. Sirow

ISBN: 978-1-969021-26-8 (ebook)
ISBN: 978-1-969021-25-1 (Paperback)
ISBN: 978-1-969021-27-5 (Hardcover)

# Acknowledgement

This book would not have been written, but for my daughter, Adelle!
- Love You A!

# Preamble

The first 24 years of my life were without the word "condominium." Even my teachers, friends, relatives, and others never spoke the word or knew of it! Yet, for the next 50 years plus, the word "condominium" was a large part of my life and spoken by and to me almost daily.

At the young age of 23, I was introduced to the profession of property management as a career. A property manager is an individual or entity hired by the property owner to oversee and manage the daily workings of their real estate investment.

My exposure to property management began during my college years when I became an assistant manager at a 22-unit student housing apartment complex in Kent, Ohio. At first my responsibilities were limited to manual labor only, then I became the manager, and my career began.

It was not until 5 years later that I was introduced to condominium management in all aspects.

This book is written for others to avoid the years of learning curve that I had to transition to fully understand the word "condominium." Condominium, by definition, is a simple word, but daily practical living and buying is very complex.

# C

## The Dark Side of Condominiums

One definition of a condominium is a community of people with similarities in economic and social well-being anchored into apartment living, but with the exception that they own their real estate home.

Legal, professional, and scholars will define condominium living from an aspect that narrates to a definition that facilitates the benefits of their employment.

Condominium living is not for everyone, as the main common denominator is to have an economic position that allows for the unknown and all that will be imposed upon one as a condominium victim. These victims live under an undemocratic rule. These victims live under the control of a smaller group of condominium individuals that, like many other controlling entities, become self-serving to their own individual likes, dislikes, and whims. These individuals impose control on all. They impose their interest upon their victims who accept all with no or limited explanations to their demands. This smaller group of individuals is commonly referred to in condominium living as "The Board."

A belief in transparency is not a prerequisite to becoming a board member or becoming a condominium victim. Victimization is by choice. One does not want to expose and the victim prefers not to want to know. Victims buy into a "lifestyle" to be without issues or problems.

The blame for victimization lies solely with the victims. It is not that they have faith in the board. They prefer not to know. It is not until a momentous budget increase or a significant special assessment is placed before them that they take the initiative to inquire into the reason thereof.

They may complain about this or that, about the board's actions, among themselves, but not to board members. They remain content and submissive until the board's financial stipulation disrupts their personal economics. Some are unable to pay and are then forced into foreclosure.

Boards are resistant, if not outright refuse to increase condominium expenses to owners. First and foremost, they also must pay this increase themselves as a wonder and compel their neighbors and condominium friends also to do so. It is only when no alternatives are available to them, and many wait years beyond. With this, procrastination leads to inflationary increases and potential additional damages, e.g., roof leaking repair. These additional expenses are only known to the board and contractors, as the owners remain uninformed.

The same condominium owners can remain on the board indefinitely. They advance their positive accomplishment while dismissing negative issues, if known to the ownership, would be labeled as negligence. Board knowledge is similar to a black hole with only knowledge in it.

The board gets reelected by three factors: 1) owners' perception of board members historical experiences, 2) what is promoted by a board member to the ownership as to their accomplishment, and 3) the most credence factor for reelection is to obtain as many voting proxies from owners who do not attend the annual meeting to elect officers. With these proxies all board members vote for themselves and each other. This assures each board position into perpetuity regardless of the owner perception or a board member's accomplishment or lack thereof.

# C

The company had foreclosed on a 20-story apartment complex consisting of approximately 300 units. We believed such apartments could be a perfect candidate for a condominium conversion.

In a foreclosure, all previous debt is "washed away" except for taxes and other loan liens. My company had a second mortgage lien on this property, so we were next in line for ownership.

My job was to meet with individual contractors on site and pay them ten cents on the dollar for their work performed on the building, although we owed them nothing as a result of the foreclosure. We wanted to make a positive impact in the community and to have a relationship with contractors, as the need may further arise.

We set up at the building a waiting room, my office and an office for our legal counsel, by which he would have contractors sign-off as to the ten-cent agreement. After 7 contractors, all was going well until I met with a contractor who performed the excavation for the building foundation.

After I made my proposal for 10 cents, he sat there, looked at me eye to eye, and said nothing. After about 1 minute of complete silence by both of us (seemed like years), he reached off to his right side, pulled out a gun, and set it on the left side of my desk. Again, he still did not say anything! After seeming like more years, he pointed to a window behind him without turning around. He looked at me, eye to eye, and finally said, "Do you see the bulldozer on that truck?" I looked out the window and answered, "Yes." He then said, "If I raise my right hand, that bulldozer comes off the truck and takes this building down - do you understand me?" I again looked out the window, at the gun, and back at him - he was partially smiling. He then said that he did all the work per his contract and did not give a damn about the legalities or foreclosure, and he wanted 100% of the

5

money owed to him. I immediately completed the paperwork at 100% payment to him, handed it to him, and told him to go to the next office, and our attorney would finalize the transaction. Within moments, I received a phone call from our attorney stating that such was not our policy or plan. I indicated I would explain later, and as he countered with "but, but," I hung up the phone and continued with additional contractors.

When I returned to the home office on Monday morning, the same attorney, plus two others, and the president, were waiting for me in the president's office. Our upper management was upset because our agreement with the 100% payment was against our earlier company plans and would set a precedent for the company on all future events.

After I explained the details of this contractor with the gun, stare down, and the bulldozer, they all stood up, shook my hand, and said, "Well done!"

## C

The company foreclosed on a condominium community on the edge of the St. Croix River. The river froze to the extent that cars would drag race on the ice as if there was no tomorrow. Being from the Midwest and adjacent to Lake Erie, I always found their events interesting but dangerous. The community consisted of 32 upscale, huge units overlooking the river with a variety of boats as a front yard. We retained a marketing firm to provide high-end brochures, news releases, and prepare two sales model units.

Approximately 45 days after the marketing firm completed this assignment, we received an invoice for $48,000. Our first reaction was that it was expensive, but to give them the benefit of doubt, we scheduled a meeting with the owner of the marketing firm.

We met in a hotel conference room just outside of St. Croix. There were approximately 12 separate invoices without backup details for the work involved. In the meeting, the first 5 invoices went smoothly, with adequate explanation provided by the owner, and we immediately accepted the information and documented each invoice. Commencing with the 6th invoice, the owner appeared agitated and asked if this was "really necessary." I responded that our accounting department requested this task of me to assign different accounting codes per each invoice. He appeared to have understood this explanation until the 7th invoice and began to talk with a raised voice. I attempted to calm him down, but he would not hear of it. With the 8th and 9th invoices, he merely stated, "change the amount to anything you want." I explained the purpose of the meeting was not a question of dollar level, but to provide explanations to the invoice. He responded with, "I just want out of here." With the 10th and 11th invoices and him sitting quietly with no response, I offered my best explanation and, with each invoice, adjusted the dollar amount lower from his invoice, hoping he would realize the magnitude and the impact of his insane behavior - he did not! By the end of the 12th invoice, I again offered an explanation and adjusted the invoice lower by 90%. I again asked him if this met with his approval of my provided explanations and difference against his invoiced amounts. He said, in a highly explosive voice, "Yes, and let me get out of here!" I requested he provide a sign-off approval on all 12 invoices for his approval of which he did. When I returned the invoices to our home office accounting department, they expressed appreciation for the additional detailed explanation of the invoices and said they would process them immediately.

They lastly looked at the total adjusted approved dollar amount and stated, "Wow, what a difference, good meeting." The original invoice of $48,000 was reduced to $29,000. The greater invoice amounts were the last to be discussed, believing they would require the most time to discuss - they obviously did not.

I have repeatedly told this story to young people to teach them that regardless of the situation, "Always retain your composure regardless of what the challenges may be."

C

Our sister construction company had built a beautiful 175-unit garden condominium project in a heavily wooded forest. Every unit had a scenic view of trees, and some with also a blue water lake view.

With all units being new, with scenic views, and in a great neighborhood, we all believed such to be a quick and easy sellout.

However, because of the high interest rates and a glutton of condominium units on the market at the time, said units were not selling. After about 18 months and only 17 units having been sold, the company instructed me to buy-back the 17 units and convert the community to an apartment housing only; the condominium conversion could come later.

With the 17 units being sold, these owners realized their financial investment would be stagnant and difficult to resell if the balance of the community was all rental apartments. The first 14 units were an easy buy back as we desperately wanted to make this an apartment community. We also offered a generous financial buy-back package of all reimbursement of improvements they may have made, relocation costs, loan penalties, and fees associated with early termination or legal fees they may occur. All expenses were to be paid by our company. These costs ranged from $5,000 to $20,000 per unit.

The last unit was the most difficult. He was single, almost at retirement age, and was difficult with the neighbors. Also, he would not return calls or respond to our mailings. Finally, a local broker and I were able to get an appointment with him on a beautiful fall sunny midafternoon day.

When we knocked on his door, he came to the partially open door and told us to wait outside in the hall as he was shaving. After approximately 15 minutes, he allowed us in, pointed to a sofa, and told us to sit. He then read from his notes and stated the three things he must have for the buy-back. He stated that there was no negotiation, no further discussion - this is it! He then read from his notes:

1. $10.00 off of his monthly rent for two years.
2. An assigned parking space with his name on it in front of his unit.
3. Not to contact him unless it was an emergency.

I asked if the three items were all of his demands, and he stated, "Yes, take it or leave it." The broker and I looked at each other and said we need to obtain upper management approval to his demands and excused ourselves to the hallway. As we walked out the door, he again stated, "Gentleman, this is a take it or leave it deal." In the hallway, we both looked at each other and broke into laughter, as this meant for us:

1. No improvement reimbursement.
2. No loan or legal fees
3. No relocation costs.

When we reentered the unit, he stated in a gruff voice, "There is no need to sit down; do we have a deal or not?" We told him that he left us with no place to go and he made it very clear of his demands, and yes, we have a deal. We thanked him for his time and consideration and would have the appropriate documents back to him shortly.

I immediately contacted our home office legal counsel to expedite all legal documents with his demands. They kept asking me, "Are you sure this is it? Are you sure?" I stated I was very sure because of the repetition of his three items. The next morning, I hand-delivered such to him, he signed, and we had a deal.

## C

Although the construction crew of a condominium conversion was to commence work at 8:00 a.m., Monday through Friday, they could not be found until 8:45 a.m. each day. It was at that time that all crew members would appear instantly.

One day, while walking through a hallway, I overheard a worker say to another, "See you at 8:00 a.m. again in unit 412," and they both giggled.

The next day at about 8:15 a.m. I went to unit 412 and saw all the workers looking earnestly through a window in the opposite direction. None appeared to notice or care that I was in attendance, as they were silent and smoking intensely.

As I looked in the same direction across the way into an adjoining window of the C-shaped building, I could see a woman taking a shower with a full floor-to-ceiling window. She kept smiling and waving across the way to her audience. I then stated in a commanding voice, "This party is over, you are being paid to be here!" The room vacated abruptly, leaving behind a room full of smoke and hundreds of cigarette butts. The same day, the locks were changed on this unit, and it was the last to be renovated.

## C

We had begun sales on a condominium conversion from apartments to condominiums of 74 units in Washington, DC.

On a Saturday, I visited the community to inspect the progress of our construction company with unit improvements.

Upon entering the main entrance, I was greeted by a journalist from a local paper. He indicated he was to do an article on condominium conversions and asked if I could assist him. I responded gladly, and receiving the publicity could only help sales.

All went well, then he stated, "off-the-record," and proceeded to ask a question. In my reply, I used the word "damn" jokingly.

Early the next morning, I received a call from my angry boss, who read to me my "quote" using the word "damn" from a local paper. He was upset, along with our parent company, a major American steel company. The boss indicated the parent company was advised through a newspaper search firm of my quote. The search firm's responsibility was to research all newspapers and magazines in the United States and foreign countries and report wherever the parent company's name was used.

I have not used the word "damn" in my remaining life - "off the record" lesson learned.

## C

Our company was one of the first to convert apartments to condominiums in Washington, D.C. My responsibility was to contact building apartment renters and convert them to buyers.

Our sister company would then perform all necessary construction improvements. This formula was successful in these condominium conversions.

Each Friday after work, the construction superintendent and I would have drinks at a local pub to review the past week and plan for the next. After one such meeting, he explained his wife's full time job was to transfer cash in an upscale shopping bag from lobbyists to senators and congressmen/women.

She was chosen as she was elegant, poised, dressed well, did not ask questions, well spoken, did not take any of the money, and could pass most personnel to make her deliveries.

C

The condominium bylaws clearly state.......... additions, alterations, or improvements......... the cost of which exceeds $3,000....... Shall be approved by unit owners to exercise not less than a majority of voting power prior to the board proceeding with.......

The additions, alterations, and improvements to building common areas were made by the board without any approval or knowledge by the ownership as to the costs, actual costs were just under $125,000. The ownership, although paid for all through their monthly fees, was none the wiser!

C

A board member had assisted the board in securing recommendations for insurance coverage for the community and board coverage. All board members had approved his recommendations for the prior years. Through an email to the insurance agent requesting a commission, he mistakenly also forwarded the same email to the community manager.

The manager, not sure how to interpret such, forwarded the email to the community's legal counsel. The legal counsel responded that in the email, it appears the board member was earning a commission for his assistance to the board. The legal counsel stated he would discuss the email with the board and advise. Days later, the legal counsel stated the board did not wish to pursue, although deceived about the commission for possibly several years, as this was against board policy. The ownership was none the wiser.

## C

A board member was celebrating at a party in the community's party room on the weekend. Upon inspection on the following Monday, it was noted the room had been trashed. The board member denied any culpability for the trashing and was supported by fellow board members.

Upon viewing a video of the party, both the board member and board members humbly retracted their comments as they had forgotten about the video camera in the room. The board members only paid for partial repairs and cleanup.

The balance was paid for through the ownership money fees, and they were none the wiser.

## C

Some board members are notorious for requesting priority of services or to be paid by the community when, in fact, it is a member's financial responsibility.

Example: A board member demanded, although the landscaper was working on a common area of the community, that the landscaper be pulled off and transferred to his condominium unit to do like work - now! The manager directed the landscaper to the board member's unit later in the day. The landscaper returned to the common area the next day to complete their work.

Example: Major deck repairs were being made throughout the property. As owner requests were made, each was given priority in the order received. A board member demanded to be moved up on the list ahead of others. The board member was moved to the top and repairs were then completed to other owners. The following year, the repairs proceeded with the same board member demanding to be moved from ninth on the priority list to first, and the management again complied.

Other owners on the list were none the wiser.

Many board members believe special attention should be given to their situation at any given moment. They believe their time and effort is given to the ownership as a board member and thus entitles them to demands for a priority position.

## C

Our sister company was constructing a condominium community in Washington DC from the ground up. We were in need of a marketing company to prepare brochures, TV ads, furniture models, etc. Three companies were selected to get proposals.

Three employees from the sister company and two from the management company were to evaluate and select the chosen company. This consisted of one female and four males.

The first two proposals went very well, and either could be selected. The third presentation was by a middle-aged lady. The first two used easels for their presentations. The middle-aged lady had spread all of her company exhibits on the floor in front of her and kneeled over them, and she spoke softly, pointing to each. It should be added here that she had ample breasts that were visually exposed.

After all the presentations, we convened in the conference room to discuss the presentations. When a vote was taken, it was three against two to select the middle-aged woman's marketing company. The three were all males in favor of the presentation on the floor. This company was then retained as the company to market the condominium community.

At an open house celebration of the condominium upon its construction completion, the middle-aged lady explained she was not an employee of the company selected but was under contract to make presentations throughout the United States and was very successful.

## C

Many board members become members because they have a void in their lives, whatever it may be. Their mission is not always as righteous as a teacher, doctor, or clergy member may choose. It is, as a board member once stated, "A person becomes a member to satisfy a need that is not being addressed by others," whatever that need may be - ego, respect, affection, feeling of being wanted or needed. Many of these lack-there-ofs can be voided upon retirement, whereby all needs are being met. Some may be a result of a neglectful childhood.

It is for this reason that all ownerships should stay connected and informed by board actions, as many are not the best at long-term benefits intended financial or otherwise.

## C

It was a cold, icy, blustery February day, and weather conditions were not favorable in Ohio. A woman in her early 80s had ventured to retrieve her automobile in front of the high-rise condominium community. The open-air parking lot was icy and had strong, blowing winds. Before she made it to her automobile, she fell to the ice-covered concrete. We had previously plowed and applied a heavy spread of salt as an extra precaution against the existing weather extremes. Other owners safely maneuvered to the same parking lot. She sued us and requested a jury trial against our insurance provider.

With the weather conditions noted at the trial and her reasoning for attempting to battle the elements that day to meet her hair appointment, we felt comfortable in our defense. We lost, and the jury awarded her $25,000 in damages.

Upon her return to the condominium community later that morning, she was observed with her usual walk to retrieve her mail. This was in contrast to her sitting in a wheelchair being pushed into the courthouse earlier to give her testimony.

15

# C

Condominium conversions became popular in the 1970s and 1980s. Companies would buy down low interest rates to entice apartment residents to buy their units along with an attractive sales price. The apartment residents could remain in their unit or move into another unit if they chose. They would become an owner with all the benefits of unit appreciation and tax benefits.

Some conversions were not successful as a result of the quality of the apartment or bad performance by the marking and/or sales efforts.

A high-rise apartment building in a major city was to be converted. For reasons unknown, the sales slowed down to the point of cancellation of the sale conversion.

The building became a partial apartment and a partial condominium. When a condominium owner attempted to sell their unit, the pending owner could not obtain a mortgage because of the high ratio of the apartment status. Many foreclosures were a result of the mixture of apartments and condominiums. The building, over time, reverted back to an apartment community.

# C

Capital condominium improvement is a separate account to which the ownership contributes, and it is titled a reserve account. The two most common methods of this account are:

a. The amount of the reserve is established in the budget preparations for the subsequent year and subsequently collected monthly from the ownership. It is set aside and noted in each month's computations of monthly financial statements.

This monthly statement generally is not distributed to the ownership but is entitled to them upon request. Although available to the owner, most owners do not request it.

The board generally is not bound on any given items to spend this reserve unless noted early to the ownership, so in many ways, such funds are at the pleasure of the board. Additionally, when an owner may sell their unit, all their reserves contributed are left behind with the association.

b. An alternative is a program titled "pay as you go." With this program, the ownership should individually set aside an amount with the anticipation of major repairs/improvements to be requested by the board at any given time. Some owners may have the financial wherewithal to be financially secure enough to pay any amount at any given time.

The title implies that the board requests payment for a repair/improvement as the needs arise. The board in its request to the ownership, must provide details of the particulars for the request of monies needed. This allows the ownership to question or challenge the given requested monies. Ownership may also be given permission to make payments over time, depending on the time frame required to implement the repairs/improvements.

## C

There are three entities by which a condo community can be managed:

a. Board Management:

i. Under this method, all issues are directed to the board of directors, with the board making decisions on each.

This is the least desirable as the board must pass judgment on issues relating to themselves, friends, and contractor relatives. This style quickly leads to a "secretive" style of management and very much self-serving.

b. Property Manager:

    i. This method of management employs an individual as a property manager. All issues are received by the individual who then either resolves the issue or, depending on the issue, refers the issue to the board or the community's legal counsel.

    This individual should not be a board member for the reasons noted in the above items.

c. Outsource Fee Management Company:

    i. Communications are less direct, as requests by the ownership must be directed via email or an answering service.

    If the issue is board-related, several layers of interpretations can be required and/or not received on a timely basis.

    The interest of management becomes that of the management company, which may not always be the same of the community. This can be significant as it is related to resolving issues and the communication format.

## C

Our sister construction company had built an up-scale condominium community of 34 units in Toledo, Ohio. The community was in a beautiful area with mature oak trees throughout. Sales were quickly being obtained, and everyone believed for a quick sellout.

The architect had changed the standard specs for construction. Instead of separate 4x8 sheets of plywood on all second level units, he specified all joints to glue together. This benefit reasoning was never determined.

As owners began to occupy units, management immediately received comments from the ground floor owners of excessive sounds from the second-level owners; it was only noted as they walked across the floors.

Upon several trials and errors, it was discovered that the excessive sounds resulted from the glued joints creating a "drum" effect and amplifying the foot traffic to the units below.

Eighteen units had been sold on the 2nd level. Management retained companies to resolve this issue. One to remove all owner furniture, two to remove and replace carpeting, tile, or wood flooring, and three to cut the glue joint, so that each 4x8 sheet of plywood would allow independent separation from each other.

As noted each effort required a great deal of coordination between each contractor, management, and owners as to particular time frames.

The architect absorbed all expenses involved in his experiment of glued flooring joints.

## C

Our real estate company was owned by a major steel company. They also owned the company that built apartments and condominiums, and our company would then oversee. We considered the construction company our sister company and worked closely with them.

They had constructed an up-scale condominium community of 32 units. The three areas of construction defects were immediately noted:

a. The second-level floors of the townhomes sloped noticeably. Potential customers immediately noted this condition. Women would take out their round lipstick tube, place it on the floor, and the tube would roll to the opposite side of the room.

b. The construction company failed to waterproof the exterior cinder block walls. The basement wall would leak profusely. The construction company was attempting to resolve this at the fastest pace. However, the individuals who had purchased and occupied their units became impatient and understandably so. They constantly were in communication with management to resolve this issue.

   Their patience and legal threats resulted in the owners posting huge lemon designs on their double garage doors. Needless to say, the sales could not procure a sales positive position, and as a result, the sales stopped.

c. A contractor was retained to inject a hollow rod into the exterior landscape adjacent to the basement walls. The tube would then be injected with a protective sealing coating to the walls and prevent further leaks.

   On a spring afternoon, while receiving an updated sales report from the staff, I took a break and stepped onto the ground-floor cement patio. My foot accidentally tripped over a small cement plug that was to fill the hole the tube passed through underneath. My shoe dislodged the plug, and it popped out.

   The plug revealed a hole approximately 1/2 inch deep in the concrete patio slab of 4 inches thick. All plugged holes were inspected with the same shallow defective repair results.

## C

Board executive meetings are strictly for attendance by board members and those invited, such as the association's legal counsel. These meetings are where the most important decisions are made for the association. Owners are not invited, and the meeting minutes are not available to owners or others.

All decisions made are not recorded in the minutes and are retained in the management files. Most discussions are not legally recorded to avoid exposure to a later legal request or subpoena.

General meetings are open to the ownership, with board members and owners in attendance. These are scheduled by the board as they believe they need to be. The board addresses the owners by updating them on various issues and providing a financial community status. The meeting is then open to the ownership for questions and discussion. Ownership comments are individual issues of which is not the intent of the meeting. Such individual issues are to be addressed outside of the meeting with either a board member or management.

The purpose of the meeting is to address the "big picture" issues affecting the association as a whole. These meetings, if not controlled by the board, quickly get out of hand and are either called to adjourn or to request a police presence.

Boards today have learned to have Zoom meetings as there is less attendance by the ownership (especially mature owners), are easy to control, and quicker to adjourn. However, they are not an effective communication channel in fairness to all owners that prefer live human interaction.

## C

A board member would announce upon meeting a contractor in his unit, "I am a board member," before any other greeting.

This member would, upon completion of the contractor work, find minor flaws in the work. He then refused to pay the contractor. The contractor would then negotiate a lesser contract amount or write-off his cost. The contractor did not want to be placed on a "do not call list."

The board member could not understand why contractors would not meet to view his additional repair needs.

### C

Successful condominium boards rely upon the association's legal counsel for guidance. This can be for interpreting the association's documents or providing a legal opinion in a situation arising from an owner, contractor, or government entity.

Legal counsel frequently responded to a board request, "Where do you want to end up?" Counsel's responsibility is "to get the board there " in order to retain favorable employment with the board.

In order to get the board there, counsel often takes the board's position to the legal maximum level. This may be by way of a legal opinion, to the edge, or over the edge. Almost always, the opposing party accepts this interpretation. They know refuting this interpretation to the edge or over is not worth the potential expense or time.

Board legal counsels also rely upon their historic relationships with those who may also pass on their legal opinions within the systems to grant them an edge in an actual court legal determination.

### C

A severe hail storm had caused extensive damage to both the owner and the associated property in Ohio.

Within a week, the out-of-state insurance company sent out two representatives to inspect the damages. We began with a tour by walking on various roofs throughout the community.

The representative stated upon inspecting the damaged shingles, "repairs to those that were damaged, would be limited to only replacement."

That evening, I reviewed the entire insurance policy and noted a provision regarding shingle roof damage. The provision provided for an appearance provision. It stated that if the insured was not satisfied with the appearance of the repairs, alternative repairs were to be required.

The following day, I contacted the insurer and advised of the appearance provision. They indicated they would review the policy again. Within a week, they responded after a review they would replace all roof shingles. They then inspected the entire property and were overly generous in the coverage. The shingle replacement alone was $850,000.

## C

We were in need of staff for several condominium communities of conventional and newly built condominium buildings.

In Washington DC, competing with the federal government for employees proved to be challenging. This was most notable when soliciting for secretarial help.

Our pay range for this position was $30-$35,000 per year. The government's range was $50-$60,000, with great benefits for our like positions.

When we interviewed for this position, the applicants who applied were making the government salary. We would suspiciously inquire as to their motivation to seek a job opportunity with less salary and drastically limited benefits.

The response was universal: "we want to be busy and challenged daily."

Upon hiring these applicants, they proved to be some of the best employees in the company.

## C

All the up-scale condominium community units had a great view of the lake. In order to accomplish this feat, the developer had to lower the ground elevation on which units were to be built.

With this soil removed it allowed the remaining soil to become closer to the shale location. This would later affect three units to be constructed on the same location.

Shale, by its nature, expands and contracts as it reacts to moisture; more moisture and it expands; dry conditions, it contracts.

After approximately ten years of the 3 units being sold and occupied, the interior of the units became of concern. Cracks developed at doors and window frames, concrete slabs on ground level had risen, and walls bowed in or out.

The community declaration stated the structural components include.... foundations.... located on the exterior of individual units .....and are common areas, per the declaration. Common area expenses are to be those of the association and not the owner's responsibility.

When the condition was first reviewed by the on-site manager and in conjunction with the community declaration, he advised this issue would be that of the association expense.

It was further reviewed by the association's legal counsel, and he noted state law superseding the community declaration indicated that unless conditions are a safety concern, such would be a homeowner's financial responsibility.

The owner met with the board, manager, and legal counsel for the association expense, but the board rejected the owner's position.

The owners financial shale expenses for their units ranged from $30,000 - $50,000 per unit.

C

Monday through Friday our maintenance supervisor, head of housekeeping, and I would meet in the management office. We would recap yesterday and plan for the days ahead. We did this formally for 15 years.

The conversation after this practice would float off to any subject. Most times we would discuss personal items about our children, spouses, grandkids, etc. We evidently knew about each other better than our spouses, closest relatives, or friends. We covered all situations.

What I came to realize with time was a bond that became indescribable. Even to this day, I cannot place a label on it: major respect, affection, closeness, love - something!

This was not duplicated in my entire business career and I was very fortunate to have this experience one time!

C

Board Members Must Have to/Must Not on a Board

a) Single moms with teenage children must have: seen and heard it all, be passionate, caring, and can deal with teenage behavior displayed by the community owners at times.

b) Engineer - must not: regardless of the situation, have an adamant answer for all, whether they have knowledge of the subject or not.

c) Small business owners must have: has experience with all plumbing and electrical.

d) Legal/Accounting must not: view all aspects of a situation in a narrow, related professional view of situations, and must not have another discipline in evaluating situations.

e) Clergy must not: view each situation only in its positive aspects, not its down sides, and only its futuristic positive, regardless of what the board discusses. This does not provide balance to the evaluation.

f) Retired members must have: certainly have time to research, discuss, and evaluate to provide guidance to the board.

g) Politicians must not: get any response that is popular at the time.

h) Financial members must not: do not relate to the human side of situations; all evaluations must be presented from the monetary perspective.

i) Members owning condominiums must not: always make comparisons to their other condominium ownership, "while at (fill in any place) this is how to deal with" condominiums are much like people's personalities, all unique in some way, but yet not.

j) Teachers must have: discipline, learn to think before speaking so as not to be challenged, do research on the subject, stay calm, be willing to compromise to settle disputes, and see all sides.

k)  Medical must have: understand the real issues of life, can read community issues in perspective, speak from experience, not be quick to judge, and quickly call out false statements.

l)  Military members must: have high discipline, must follow Robert's Rules of Order, read and adhere to all community documents, no deviation, evaluate comments from titles of those speaking and not on facts, intimidating, personally being presented.

m)  Young members must have: willing to learn, open to all ideas, express in an articulate manner, open to criticism, willing to compromise, good at establishing positive relationships, research, and always prepared.

n)  The therapist must be: great at keeping situations simple, can break down issues to their lowest denominator, people deeply listen, the room becomes quiet, usually either close or correct to situations.

## C

The ladder provided access to a lake beach and boat dock area. As the lake continued to rise, the beach was lost, but the boat owner's access remained. All of them thought the lake would recede, and everything would return to normal.

The declaration states......by a positive vote of unit owners.... not less than (70%) ......determine.... property is obsolete.... damaged.... the board shall.... proceed with rehabilitation.

One member of the board decided against the boat owners and advised management to remove the ladder, the balance of the ownership was none the wiser.

# C

Pigeons have a reputation of being messy birds, our condominium building was no exception to them.

The exterminator made several recommendations for placing artificial snakes, dogs, cats, and spikes. We tried all but to no avail. We were at a loss.

The exterminator recommended we contact a nearby condominium building, as they had found a solution. We immediately did so.

We scheduled an on-site meeting with the manager to tour his location. We were impressed by their solution. They had built a small frame structure on the building's roof. After which, they purchased 8 falcons to control their pigeon issue. The roof housing was an environment for the pigeons not to leave.

As we toured the community, we noted out of the hallway windows, the dead carcasses on window ledges were feathers, guts, and blood—the remains of the falcon control effects. Because the building was a 25-story high-rise and the windows were secured, there was no way to clean the pigeon remains.

The manager indicated that the residents, employees, and guests were extremely upset about this condition. The manager stated they did not have a solution and would have been grateful to return to the simple pigeon problem that we were experiencing.

When we inquired, "Why not just remove the falcons and their nests?" He indicated the animal protection agency had classified falcons as a protected species, and they could not.

So glad we had scheduled a tour of this Ohio property.

## C

Unless strict condominium laws are passed within the next 25 years, condominiums, as we know today, will be limited to only the affluent, wealthy, privileged, and rich. The best of automobiles, housing, medical treatment, and the legal system have all transitioned from the average American to the benefit of the upper American.

When available, people's weaknesses prevail for all groups of people. Yes, there are exceptions, but they are very limited. One only has to watch the news or read the newspaper to add support to this observation. People make decisions on "What I am going to gain or what am I going to lose."

Board of directors of condominiums are no different and even more likely to support this claim. Within a group setting, one attempt to establish a "right" position to a situation where one or more on the board members have an opposing position is virtually impossible. There are always more arguments against doing the "right" than for it. The validity does not have to connect, only close.

Opposing comments generally are supported with aggressive speech, words, and gestures. We capitulate to the speaker of such behavior.

Boards operate within the scope of the above, and perhaps all boards do, regardless of corporate, political, or community levels. They do because all are dominated by human behavior.

Boards are heavily protected legally and by what the given ownership does not know. Boards control all information.

## C

An elderly woman visited the office to explain she had just driven through our 4-foot-high wall on the second-level parking lot. She indicated her accelerator was stuck and that she was very sorry.

After approximately two weeks of getting the car bodywork and repaired, she again visited the office. She explained that on the previous Sunday, her accelerator again stuck, and she just missed hitting people in the church parking lot.

Without her consent, we contacted her major car manufacturer and explained all events to them. They were extremely appreciative.

Within one week, they contacted her and exchanged the automobile for her. She received the latest model with all added features.

She visited the office and could not thank us enough!

## C

It was my first phone call on a cold winter day. The caller, without an introduction, just stated, "We want your side of the story." My response was to back up the conversation with who is calling, why calling, and what this is about.

The caller explained that he was a reporter with the major newspaper in the city and was calling in regard to an issue that had occurred on Sunday, the previous day. He indicated that a woman who was also in our condominium building as a potential purchaser was assaulted by a prominent lady while in the hallway. The lady who committed the assault was the wife of a prominent car dealership owner in northern Ohio.

The caller explained the potential purchaser was with her broker looking to purchase a unit within the building when she was approached by a lady screaming, "we don't need your kind in the building." The purchaser was a lady of color.

The caller indicated that the assaulting lady proceeded to lash the purchaser with a coat hanger. The caller requested that I, as the manager, provide a response for the article he was in the process of writing for a next-day story. I asked that I be allowed to review the facts with the respective parties and contact them back. I immediately placed a call to an ex-editor of this same paper and explained the entire story to him and explained the building could not afford such a story. He stated he understood and would see what he could do.

Later the same afternoon, he contacted me and said because of past favors owed him at the paper, he was able to "kill the story," I expressed my extreme gratitude and then indicated I now owed him a favor.

Within a week he took me up on my "favor" offer. He stated in his call he had fallen and needed a ride to the emergency center. I obliged, and after his medical care, I then drove him back to his home.

Three days later, he again called and indicated he had to go to the grocery store and asked that I take him. I explained the emergency ride was an exception, but I would not take him grocery shopping. It was against company policy for liability reasons. He became angry and abruptly hung up the phone. He then called three additional times with the same request. Each time, I indicated I would not for the same reasons and suggested he contact a cab service. He indicated they were too expensive. He was known in the building for being extremely cheap.

As an example: upon returning to the building after having breakfast, he burst into my office saying, "George, George, look at this receipt, it's only $2.13!" He indicated it "would have been much more had I not taken my own toast!" I complimented this invoice amount and a "good move on the toast." He went out the door.

Approximately 6 months later he again called and needed a ride to pick-up medicine as he could no longer drive his automobile. I again suggested a cab or have them deliver the meds. He quickly responded that both alternatives were too expensive. I again stated I would not take him.

Within minutes, he was in my office, screaming and berating me as a manager. I asked that he sit down, and I closed the door. I stated we all knew he had money and that he should spend it while he was alive. He had no remaining family members. He then became very emotional and spoke in a whisper. He indicated he wished he had traveled in his retirement years, and yes, he could afford to do so. However, at his current age and medical conditions, he could not. He then pulled up his pant legs and showed me the size of his calves. They were 3 times bigger than normal.

A sad story and a lesson.

## C

A 7th-grade class of students changed my career path.

I graduated from a state college with a degree in education, being one of nine children, the first to graduate, and with honors.

After graduation, as a state requirement, one has to do student teaching at some level. My assignment was a 7th-grade class at a local school. My anxiety and fear matched my enthusiasm. I wanted to do well and commit to a career in teaching.

After approximately 2 weeks, my anxiety and fear exceeded my enthusiasm. The students had no bounds. The walls, ceiling, or floor could not contain their energy levels. They must have had dual ear filters to control word intake. At the end of the school year, I have to admit that they won and I lost!

After 15 years in property management, an opportunity arose as I was contacted as to an interest in teaching an adult real estate class in condominium and apartments. Without hesitation, I stated I would, as both were my specialties in management. The class was to be at a state college, all real estate adults, with approximately 20-25 students.

My confidence level was high until I walked into the room and observed the students. Most were older than me, and some I had met through earlier business dealings. My first thought was that each of their real estate experience by years alone would greatly exceed mine,

After the first class of only individual introductions by each, my thoughts of their years of experience made me realize they were beyond theory and textbook teachings.

I decided on a different approach for the class. It would be based on individual real estate experience in condominiums and apartments. All facets were to be covered.

Monday through Thursday were strictly round table discussions, with Fridays as a recap of what knowledge was obtained and how such would be implemented into the future. Outside the classroom, students developed relationships, and some deals were made.

Although the college administrator inquired about my interest in teaching additional classes, much to my regret, I had to reject the offer.

With my current job responsibilities, travel schedule, and family obligations, I did not believe I could do justice to all, and sadly, I declined.

The adult class, in part, restored my self-esteem to my educational degree that was greatly diminished by the 7th grade class.

## C

The condominium community had only 28 units, all built by our sister company. It was exclusive and in a highly wooded area. One could touch a tree while standing on one's balcony.

Sales exceeded our expectations, and we received a favorable reception from the community.

On a summer afternoon, a very poised, mature lady entered the sales office holding a poodle. One could tell the poodle meant a great deal to her because of the care and closeness she showed it while talking and all the affection she showed it. After touring a condominium unit, she stated she "loved it" and wished to purchase it.

While sitting by the desk, the salesperson reminded her that the community had a "no pet policy." When the lady inquired about what that meant, the salesperson stated, "No cats or dogs" allowed.

The lady snuggled her poodle even tighter and said she would not purchase the unit.

The salesperson calmly indicated she could; she would just have to "get rid of the poodle." The lady sat speechless, got up, and walked out the door.

We later learned through research (of which we should have done earlier) that 51% of Americans have either a pet - cat or dog. We excluded 51% of viable potential purchases - not smart!

**M**

## Other Life Experiences-Management

The company was renovating a shopping mall in West Virginia. We were to manage this $1.7 million renovation. We retained a construction management firm to redesign and obtain contractors' bids to perform the work.

Prior to finalizing the contracts, we scheduled a contractors' meeting at a local hotel for $35.00 and invited all of the contractors to attend a morning breakfast.

All contractors attended, and the simple question was, "If you were designing these renovations, what changes would you make?"

Contractors work every day with construction improvements and repairs, and from whom would be better to solicit knowledge. As an example, the construction management noted a sewer line to be L-shaped, located under the asphalt in front of each storefront. The plumber contractor indicated running these in a straight line, without the L-shape, would reduce the linear footage.

I had pages of great notes, many of which were incorporated into the final design and implemented. From an investment of a room charge of $35.00 and breakfast, final costs were reduced by $135,000 thanks to the contractors.

**M**

Our sister company was attempting to construct a government-subsidized apartment community on the east side of Toledo. The company retained a well-respected local broker to make a presentation before the local community council board for approval to commence construction. After each presentation lasting approximately one to two hours, prior to which there were 4 attempts, the council rejected each.

The broker then retained the most hippie-looking Toledo University student to attend the fifth council meeting. The meeting commenced much like the previous four, with the audience voicing comments of:

We do not want changes to our neighborhood because of the people who occupy these units:

a) abandoned cars

b) the minority will occupy due to their multitude of kids playing in the street

c) drapes blowing out of the windows

These outbursts were all the same as noted in the 4 previous meetings.

After about half an hour, the hippie joined in saying similar comments, but he added his own comments about black people in a descending, racist, aggressive way while walking around the room.

The audience sat in their seats silently. After a short time, they started to object to this hippie's comments, not wanting to be personally associated with such.

That evening, the council approved the construction of the 325-unit apartment complex, and the audience gave a standing ovation for its passage.

## M

A beautiful blue company car and had just over 72,000 miles at the end of a three-year lease. Thirty days prior to the day of its return date, a meeting with the dealership was established to review the return process. After all gentleman's greetings, a discussion followed as to wear and tear, exact return dates, etc.

When the meeting was directed to the financial amounts, the meeting took on a serious tone. Any mileage over 12,000 miles per year or 36,000 miles was to be assessed at .25 per mile. The dealership, after calculating, stated, "Wow, you are going to owe us a lot of money." I jokingly answered, "Not if you roll back the odometer." I laughed but the dealership just ignored my comment.

After the return of the car I received from the dealership an invoice and noted they had miscalculated the final invoice by $30.00, me still owning them. I waited the full 30-day due date and then advised them of this error. They apologized about their error and forwarded a correct invoice.

Again, I waited a full 30 days and stated I disagreed with the mileage they had sent. I requested to see the car again with the mileage they noted. They contacted me via the phone and advised me that the car was not available due to them not being able to locate the car.

I then recalled that my comment of a "roll back" with no laughter was perhaps only a one-sided humor.

**M**

An office building leasing agent of three urban buildings was effective and professional in her employment. She visited my office in the late afternoon.

She had a daughter who was five years old. The leasing agent had received a visit from children services, who stated that an employee at the daycare center had been accused of child molestation, and the agency wished to speak to her five-year-old daughter. The leasing agent agreed and set a date and time to do so at her home. After a visit with children services, of which they required no parent to be present, the agency notified the leasing agent that she and her husband were under investigation. The leasing agent was devastated, and as she told me the story, she began to cry. She stated that she and her husband had nothing to hide. She indicated she then went to church to pray for guidance from God for answers about her family.

Her parents had immigrated to America, and she had worked in her parents' grocery store since she was four years old, stocking shelves. Her father had questioning connections in the community, which the leasing agent attested and vowed never to be a part of or associated with as she matured.

On a late Friday afternoon, she visited the children's services agency to discuss the potential charges. The agency employee was called out of her office in the middle of their conversation. The leasing agent then noticed a paper in the children's services employees' inbox stating that the leasing agent's five-year-old daughter was to be removed from her home.

She immediately left the office, returning to the church for guidance again. The same late Friday evening, she contacted her father and explained the entire situation to him. The next day was a Saturday, and she received a telephone call at 6:30 AM from the case manager of the children services department. The case manager stated that all was good and the investigation regarding her daughter had been dismissed.

**M**

Texas always has a great deal of sunshine. The apartment community of 350 units was a middle to upscale living community. Two events that remain memorable:

a.  Our company installed window film on all southwest apartment windows to deter the harsh afternoon sun. The unit dwellers much appreciated this event and expressed gratitude to the management for the effort.

Almost immediately after, management received a visit from the local police department accusing of heavy traffic jams, and cars stopped at the area of the window film location in the evening hours. That evening, management scheduled with the police department to monitor these traffic areas. The cause of traffic concerns was quickly identified. The apartment dwellers were either nude or semi-nude within their units. When they questioned the residents as to why they would be in this state of undress in the evening hours, they stated they believed because they could not see out of the window as a result of the film that people could not see in. We then realized, in fact, that the film amplified the external view. All film dwellers were notified the following morning as to the film's transformation of images.

b.  A Texas apartment community was soliciting cable proposals as the existing contract was to expire. The manager had scheduled an evening appointment in the community center for me to meet a contractor to review the last proposal.

At approximately 8:00 PM, a gentleman and a young lady met with me. His presentation was going well with the young lady remaining silent. After about one hour, the gentleman stated he had to obtain additional information from his vehicle and departed. The young lady began to converse, asking questions of me; most notable as to my activities after this meeting and other personal concerns. All were not related to the cable proposal. After approximately 15 minutes, the gentleman returned and handed me a company brochure of which he had already provided to me at the beginning of the meeting.

The following morning, I met with the community manager and recapped with her all proposals. I also explained to her the very unusual meeting of last evening. She inquired of me, "Did

I know why the young lady was at the meeting?" I explained the most likely, to assist in the presentation. The manager indicated not so, as the young lady was retained from an escort service. The manager stated that the company has a reputation for "adding" to their proposals and then extorting an acceptance of their proposal.

A young country boy had just experienced a rarity of the business world.

## M

The National Labor Board had commissioned a lawsuit against our company and a union in Pennsylvania. The union was a smaller union company whereby our company had negotiated a contract for employees of a city office building.

The trial was extremely intense, with five representatives of the National Board and three lawyers representing our company and the union. This trial was from Monday to Friday in the month of August.

We met with our lawyers after the daily trial; we ate breakfast, lunch, and dinner together until midnight each day. I knew each question they were to ask and the answer to give. As an example, in the trial, our lawyer was in the process of asking me a question, such as if I could identify a document, as he was about to stand up 10 feet away from me; I said I could. Everyone in the courtroom laughed as I had yet to visually see the document. The lawyer said, "Let me show it to you first." I had already seen this document several, several, several times!

There was no air conditioning in the courtroom, and in August, the room became warm. After lunch, the judge would turn his chair sideways and take a fifteen—to twenty-minute nap as the trial proceeded.

On Friday, late in the afternoon, the National Board lawyer stated he had one more question for the union president. He asked the question, the union president answered, and we all had a tremendous sigh of relief; it was over. Then, the union president went on to add comments that were not part of the lawyer's questioning.

This added an additional hour of time. The lawyer discrediting the union president with additional damning questions!

Our company was found innocent of any wrongdoing. The union, however, received heavy financial penalties, which raised questions about its future existence.

**M**

The company owned a strip shopping center in South Carolina and was highly successful. Because of its success, the end store required additional parking.

A request was made to the local government committee to add this parking. In the location of the requisition were several mature trees that would require their removal. We anticipated a difficult response as the community was very strict on environmental and code restrictions. After several meetings and stressful conversations, the committee grudgingly agreed to visit the site and tag all the trees to remain. Several days after their visit and my returning to the shopping center, it was noted that all the trees were tagged.

When questioning the committee, they indicated, as earlier stated, they would "tag all trees not to be removed - and that is what they did!"

**M**

Our sister company constructed a 300-unit government-subsidized community in the state of New York.

a) A faith based organization approached us as an experiment to employ a clergy as an on-site manager. The clergy would not openly preach religion but could lead by example and display good faith with the issues which the residents were confronted with in their daily living. The clergy was trained in people issues on all walks of life and educational degrees. This proposal appeared with great promise to be of benefit to residents and our company.

At first, everything went as well as we had anticipated. However, after approximately six months, we noticed rental delinquency became a concern. In a discussion with the manager, he had a difficult motivation to enforce our rental collection policy. We attempted to continue working with him and stressed the importance of rental collections. We also began to notice that other residents who had always paid their monthly fees on time were now becoming delinquent as well. Obviously, the word was spreading throughout the community of collections not being enforced. We could not convince the clergy manager to enforce rental collections and thus had to terminate this experiment.

Had this experiment worked, it would have very easily been expanded nationally.

b) As I walked into the building, I could hear a woman scream, "If you ever touch me again, I will cut your dick off." I knew exactly who she was without even seeing her.

She was a middle-aged woman whom we had been attempting to evict for two years. She had filed complaints with every agency as to our male maintenance staff accosting her daily. We were working with her therapist to find a facility to deal with her mental condition.

She had just walked into the leasing office as I approached the door. Upon entering she introduced herself and began to plead to not remove her from the building and that she would be the "ideal resident." I indicated all was out of my control and for her to speak to her therapist. She then noted her grandson was coming home from school, she asked me to wait and that she would return.

She returned to the office and introduced her grandson to me. She explained to him that I was the gentleman that was "throwing them" out of the building.

As the office has the staff and other potential residents, I suggested we convene our discussion in the adjoining manager's office.

As she sat down, she placed her hands over her face and began to cry hysterically. She then abruptly stopped, grabbed her purse with a long leather strap, threw her metal chair aside, and started swinging at me. Though I was younger, she was faster and hit me several times with her purse.

The manager and security guard quickly entered the room and attempted to remove her. They were successful until they were by the door frame. She dug her hands and feet into the frame as they pulled her backward. She then shouted language that none of us had ever heard.

Six months later, she was escorted by the police from the building with explicit language again for all to hear.

c) The teenage boys would climb on top of our New York building roof and drink beer. After their bottles were empty, and as a contest, they would throw the bottles down at the cars below. The building was a block wide with streets off to either side.

The police would visit the management office and request our assistance. They recommended locking the roof access door. Shortly after, the city fire department visited the office and stated we could not lock the door. They indicated in case of a fire they would need the roof to remove residents from the building. The police and fire departments went back and forth for months.

Thinking it would be best to resolve this issue in a meeting, we scheduled this with the police and fire department. We met in the fire department chief's office for approximately two hours with the chief reading from a code manual stating why the doors could not be locked. With that, I left the office and proceeded to the elevator. Just before entry to the elevator, I backed away and went back into the chief's office, where the two chiefs were laughing hysterically.

The fire chief stated earlier that a ladder would be required to remove residents off the roof. When back in the room I asked him how high will your ladder rise. He indicated maybe to the 8th or 10th floor of the 20 story building on top of 4 levels of parking. I did not say anything and returned to the management office where I advised the staff to again lock the roof door. I did not hear anything from the city government agency again.

Perhaps hearing themselves speak out loud also made sense to them.

d) Prior to the commencement of occupancy, the staff visited local businesses and obtained "how-to" manuals. The businesses were very receptive and generous in providing us numerous books of all kinds. We then provided shelves, tables, chairs, and the books into a room left behind by construction to provide a resource and study room. This room was for the benefit of the young residents of the building. After months and upon a visit to this property, the manager showed me this room and explained how the teenagers piled all the books, tables, chairs, and shelves into the middle of the room and set it all on fire.

e) Every Thursday, we scheduled an electrician to rewire the trash compactor. The teenagers would take a rag, pour gasoline on it, light it, and drop it down the trash chute. This led right into the basement compactor room, the lowest level of the building.

f) We had contacted various religious denominations to visit in the evening hours to meet with residents. Many of the residents were parents of all ages and believed counseling, if required, would be of benefit to them. Residents would contact each religious denomination directly to secure an appointment. We received many compliments from both the clergy and residents.

g) When teenagers would cause issues within the building, we scheduled an appointment with the parents. Moms were the parents we would mostly meet. We would meet in their unit with the teenager in attendance. After we explained the issue concerning the teenager to one such mom, she did not say a thing, went from her chair, walked to the child, and slapped the teenager in repetition: head, face, wherever.

As she returned to her seat, the teenager stared at me with tears. Their stare at me would say, "now you are really going to have issues."

The mom then apologized and said, "I can either continue to live here until I have enough money to move someplace better or remain here, and we work together."

My response always was, "let's work together."

h) We employed an on-site security guard for the apartment building. We believed because of the surrounding neighborhood, this employee would add to the safety of our residents and staff.

On one occasion, a group of young resident teenage boys confronted the guard. They all proceeded to force the guard onto the elevator to the ground-level parking garage to resolve this difference. As the elevator door opened at this lower level, the teenagers and guard were met by a group of residents waiting to enter the elevator. The teenage boys became frightened and ran to an automobile on that level. They attempted to start the car, but it would not start.

They abandoned the car, and before running off, they broke out all of the windows and exterior lights on the automobile.

The automobile did not belong to any of them. It was an elderly couple that lived in the building.

Management, at its expense, made all repairs to the automobile.

i) Being a government-subsidized building, HUD required a ratio of residency occupancy to be 1/3 black, 1/3 white, and 1/3 other.

We had a difficult time achieving this quota and pleaded with the government to remove the quota. They would not budge.

After two years, the owner of the building sent his representative to visit the building. We were losing approximately $10,000 a month after expenses.

We had three months' notice for this visit and made as many repairs as possible. As we toured the building, I attempted to explain the higher-than-normal expenses. For example, police raids, compactor fires, leasing quotas, hallway bullet hole repairs, etc. After each explanation, the representative said he "understood."

We returned to the office to review the financial loss statement. He kept repeating that he "understood." I became somewhat angry and stated that he could not understand as I do not even understand! He calmly stated, "allow me to share a story with you."

As he began to speak of a similar building in an adjoining state, I remember reading about the building in a Time Magazine in the St. Louis airport, last page, bold white picture in the middle of the page.

He went on to state some items not in the article. First of all, their guards were allowed to carry guns and have a police dog. (Our guards only carried a Billy club.) They also had to build an eight-foot-tall mote around the building with a chain link gate. They turned the dogs loose at night into the mote - no one could come in or out unless there was an emergency. Their current issue was that someone in the neighborhood was shooting at their residents and guests from an adjacent building. Their building was the lowest in the area.

After his story, I understood his "I understand" comments, and I had to admit I did not have major issues.

**M**

The company was expanding a shopping mall in West Virginia when an issue arose.

A construction structural steel union employee had fallen from a third-level structural beam onto the ground. Our company had no wrongdoing, but we owned the ground below. We were sued for negligence. Our insurance law firm contacted me and stated that the union employee wanted to settle the claim. My first response was to say, "No, we had no wrongdoing."

The law firm stated that they would send me a video showing the union employee's daily routine. Commencing in the morning, the lawyer described the video showing the employee getting out of bed using a hydraulic lift operated by a nurse. The lift then placed the employee in a wheelchair. The nurse then hand-fed him his breakfast, lunch, and dinner every day. Then, she placed him back in bed with the lift every evening.

Our law firm then asked me how I thought a jury would react to this video. I responded by saying, "settle for the best fair deal for the employee and our company.

## M

Our management company was owned by a major American steel company. My boss advised me that a board member's son from the steel company would be assisting me. My boss often reminded me that this son was related to the board member.

The son and I often disagreed as he thought being a college graduate and the son of a board member, he knew it all. Because of the son's position, I often capitulated to his input.

However, a situation arose that I could not compromise on, and I told him so. His only comment was, "We'll see." I knew what that meant: that my position was to be terminated. With a family of three children, I was extremely concerned and did not sleep well that evening. The following morning, I received a phone call from my boss and was advised that the son was no longer my assistant and relocated as an employee within the steel company. My day had just become better.

M

The company was soliciting an on-site manager for an office building. The process was to fly the applicant to the home office for the first interview and possibly a second. However, the applicant was local to the office building, and the third interview was to be at a local airport. There was a scheduled stopover for my flight and I thought it best to meet at the airport and offer employment if all went well.

The commencement of the interview meeting was better than was anticipated. However, as discussion progressed, something broke down. The applicant became more aggressive in her speech and word choice. She had to perceive the job opportunity slipping away. Was it something that I said or how I said it? She then went on to say she really, really needed the job as she was going to divorce (she had yet to tell her husband), and she had two young daughters. I indicated my connecting flight was about to board and that I would contact her again.

As I began to walk away, she commented, "I need the job, and if you want to get kinky, that would be okay with me."

Everyone in the immediate area looked at me, and then at her, then back at me. Needless to say, my feet moved quickly toward my gate.

As I have told this story numerous times to friends and family, obviously, they say, "well?" I merely responded by stating, "she started on Monday." (She did not!)

M

The best regional manager our company in Denver, Colorado employed oversaw 3 office buildings.

He was devoted, intelligent, strong in managing knowledge, and worked well with our home office.

He would visit the building at 4:00 - 5:00 AM to ensure the buildings were acceptable to tenants for their daily arrivals. He would return home and report back to his office at the scheduled time.

The only issue he had was controlling his temper. He would violently explode over the most minor issues. This would occur when he did not have his way or firmly comprehended a subjective opinion.

He would walk out of the room shouting his opinion, scream at those using foul language, and openly mock those in an open-attendance meeting.

We had attempted to work with him only on this issue, thinking that if we could resolve it, we would have a great employee.

We thought a visit to discuss this drawback would be best if we met at his office, perhaps a more comfortable place for discussion.

Within the meeting, he was receptive to our discussion of therapy for him at our expense. We were encouraged.

He then noticed a delivery man delivering yellow telephone books to tenants of the building. The man was heading toward the elevator. The man should have used the back door of the building and not the front door of which he had.

The regional manager jumped from behind his desk, as his office was completely enclosed in glass, and began shouting. The delivery man froze along with a multitude of others in the lobby areas.

It was at that moment we realized his behavior could not be transformed by us or therapy.

In the afternoon of the same day, after discussion with our home office, we terminated him.

## M

A major oil company club tenant invited the president of our company to an annual membership meeting of their club.

Although they had several prior annual meetings, this was our first invitation, and we felt honored.

After a short introduction with members, a very attractive young lady started to spend time with me. I was impressed as no one else, including those of my company, was with a similar person.

After about an hour, she excused herself and stated her boss wished to speak to her. She never returned. I did note that she was now spending time with my boss.

The next morning as I was going for breakfast within the hotel, she was just walking out of the hotel room of my boss.

To this day, I am not sure how she could have confused my boss and I, as we did not resemble each other at all!

## M

We had received a notice that our elevators were in violation of a new handicapped statute by the elevator servicer in our prominent downtown office building. We received proposals for this modification, and all were at an extreme expense. All the panels had to be lowered with braille signage.

We met at their office with a handicapped enforcer to seek alterations to the statute. We reviewed with them our expenses to do so. He appeared to be sympathetic to our situation.

He asked me if I noticed a "stick" in their elevator to their 4th level. We indicated we had and thought of it to be highly unusual.

He further indicated the stick was the alternative for his agency to comply with the statute.

We thanked him for his helpful suggestion and left. We did not comply with the statute on the placement of the stick. We never received a violation of the statute.

## M

A union was organizing nine employees at a West Virginia small shopping mall. We and the union were allowed to address the employees three times each. The purpose was to reply to questions and advise on the pros and cons of joining or not.

The vote was to be on a Friday. The day before, the one employee who appeared to be with management against a union organization was killed in an automobile accident. With the vote, all 8 employees were in favor of unionizing.

The union representative and I agreed to an alternate location to meet to negotiate. The employees became impatient and refused to sign union membership cards. Their signature authorized management to withhold union dues, which were then paid to the union. However, the union had to represent them on all union issues, but without getting paid to do so.

After one year the union requested out of the contract, and management refused. The union stated travel time and representation, along with not getting paid, was a losing proposition.

After two years, the employees decertified from the union with management permission. During the negotiations, the United States Labor Board had frozen all employee's wages and benefits. However, for the 2-year period, management paid the employees all back wages they would have received without a union representative.

## M

My first employment in multi-location property management was all eight out-of-town locations. We were a fee-paid management company for small investors of doctors, dentists, etc.

No overnight stays, an ok expense account, an ok company car, and consisting of apartments and a mobile home park.

The character of the company became questionable as to charges to the investors.

As their charges were being assessed to the investor, I would visit with the vice president to seek clarification on each. He would cut me off and conclude, "If you do not agree with them, then you can quit."

After approximately 5 visits with the same conclusions and not wanting to be associated with these back-charge practices, I sought other employment.

Upon his familiar "you can quit," I stood up, handed my resignation to him, and stated, "This is what I am doing now." He immediately repeated as I went to the door, saying, "Wait a minute, we can talk about this."

## M

My first call on Monday morning was from our manager, who stated our company's largest mall was under 5 feet of water. A closely located state levy had broken loose and flooded the neighborhood.

Management had to retain a helicopter service to remove customers from the roof of the mall. They were eating dinner in a restaurant located on the roof area. They refused to leave, even though they had seen the levy give way until they had completed their meal.

After 3 weeks, I visited this mall location. The state had used huge water pumps to drain the water away into a river.

Upon a visit, a front loader with me in the bucket drove through the mall - very depressing. The mall, with three major and seven other tenants, were totally void of color. The silt from the water had settled onto all merchandise with a heavy beige color. Snakes traveled ahead of us and off to the side of the front loader.

Local workers were retrieving tenant merchandise from the remaining 1 foot of water. They would store this merchandise into a 18-wheel freezer truck parked outside. The merchandise would remain frozen, then washed and sold to discount stores.

One major tenant of the 3 had a lease provision to "go dark" if they lost occupancy for more than 90 days. This meant that they could void the lease and not return to the mall. Their sales were also questionable, so this presented a challenge. We could not continue the mall without their occupancy.

With all remaining water removed, we began an interior reconstruction of the mall, commencing with the major tenant space. We did not obtain bids to do repairs, but assigned contractors to expedite the work.

Upon our home office receiving contract invoices, the account department protested them as there were not 3 competing bids as company policy. This protest was taken to the president of our company, and after hearing the accounting explanation and then mine, he merely stated, "Pay all invoices."

We were able to restore the one major tenant's space within the given lease time allotted. However, they refused to return to occupancy.

We scheduled a meeting with a state senator to assist us in their return. We scheduled an appointment and waited outside his office in a lobby reception area. This area and his office only reminded us what heaven could only look like - marble, granite, twenty-foot-high doors, leisure chairs, etc.

After a brief meeting, he advised he would consider our suggestion and get back to us. Within days he responded by stating if we were to donate money to his campaign, he would make the call without any guarantees. We did not donate, and he did not place the call. The tenant never returned to the mall. After millions of dollars in mall restoration, the mall went completely dark.

## M

My boss and I had worked together for 6 years. Another employment opportunity became available to me, which I accepted.

Upon advising my boss of this decision, he strongly suggested I remain with the company. He gave convincing reasons thereof, and I accepted them.

I then advised my future employer of my intent not to join their company. They then convinced me otherwise, and again, I accepted their offer.

After advising my decision to again leave my boss's employment, he merely stated that I was making a mistake.

Thirty days later he advised he was leaving the company for a greater opportunity. He indicated he would have recommended me for his president position if I were not leaving. My salary would have been four times my current salary.

All worked out for the both of us, as he relocated to a great state and position. I continued with my career with great related experiences and compensation.

## M

A new shopping mall had "stolen" all of our mall tenants. Ours was older and required a major renovation.

We estimated a total renovation at 7 million dollars. A component was electrical, and we received 3 proposals. These were from local contractors to the community. The proposals were $325,000, $274,000, and $76,000. All contractors received identical specifications, so these differences were of concern.

On a Friday prior to awarding the contract, each was contacted and requested they again review the specifications and their proposals; we set a deadline of 4:00 p.m. for confirmation. All confirmed their same dollar proposals before the deadline and declared their interest in doing the work again. In the conversation with the $76,000 proposal, we challenged him as to his review and his ability to do all the work conclusively. We indicated that no change orders would be permitted. He confidently stated he reviewed his proposal and, as we requested, stood behind it. Because of this vast difference, his contract was the only one we ever asked to obtain a performance bond. All electrical work was completed at $76,000 with no change order. He thanked us for the opportunity and stated a favorable profit margin.

## M

A senior golf tournament was going to be played at a local membership golf club. Name golf players were all invited. A member asked if I would be interested in volunteering. I would be a flag man, a position of which I knew nothing about. Days before the tournament all volunteers met at the club for a "dry run" rehearsal - all went well.

The day of the tournament was exciting to meet players I had only seen on TV. They were "up close," casual, and easy to communicate with about their golf world.

I was positioned on the 11th hole with a yellow flag. My responsibility was to wave the flag in the direction of the flight of the ball after it was hit by the golfer from the T-box.

I had a vision of two golf holes, the one I was positioned on and the adjacent green, a return hole.

On the return hole, one of the most renowned players had just hit his ball into a high grass area adjacent to the green.

When he struck the ball out of the grass, he blasted it into another high grass area after hitting a metal fence. He picked up his ball out of the grass, his caddy attempting to follow him, but he advised his caddy to "stay." The golfer then returned to his original grass area to replay the shot. However, he did not return his ball into the original high grass area but in the safer fairway grass.

After the tournament in which this golfer did not win, I reported this violation to the club member. I stated this violation could be viewed from a camera covering the tournament from both the T-box and the green.

The next day the member advised me they viewed this violation. I then inquired if the golfer was going to be sighted and removed from his financial winning of the tournament.

The member stated this golfer would not be, as the club did not want to bring shame to the club.

The golfer never regained his world status - karma?

## M

Maintenance equipment in our downtown highrise office building was disappearing - expensive items.

We spoke with each of the 12 maintenance employees and could not determine the thief. All equipment items were properly secured.

A polygraph agency was contacted to assist. The entire situation was explained to the president of the agency to solicit his recommendation.

He immediately recommended that each employee receive a polygraph test, but only if they agreed to it. He explained that the heavy implications of saying no to a test would suggest guilty implications. All individuals agreed to take the test.

He also indicated he would not recommend such a test to his family or friends. He stated that such a test comes with error, and if the error states guilt when, in fact, the individual was not, it would remain in people's minds, and the guilty mindset would prevail.

**M**

With a new CEO, we did not have the best chemistry. After one year, I was terminated without cause. The state has an employee-at-will provision, which allows for termination for any reason or no reason.

After 6 years of favorable reviews and performance, I felt the termination was unjust. I then filed a claim against the company.

Legal claims can proceed infinitely as opposing counsel files extensions, etc. After 2 ½ years, the company offered a settlement of $25,000.

On a misty spring day, outside of the courthouse at 6:00 PM, my counsel was pleading with me to accept the offer. He was even teary-eyed as he spoke to me. I refused, and we parted ways.

All counsel met with the judge on the day of the trial in the judge's chamber.

After 2 hours, my legal counsel approached me with an offer of $145,000 of which I accepted.

Later, I learned that the company was being taken over by a New York firm for several million dollars. They did not want to be bothered by my meager claim and told the company to resolve it quickly - and they did!

## M

We constructed a national drug store chain adjacent to our company shopping mall in West Virginia. It complimented the mall and we believed it to be an asset to the community.

After approximately 3 months, the manager of the drug store contacted us to advise that the northeast back corner of the warehouse had developed a serious split at the top.

Upon a visit within a week of the call, we noted a 2-inch split at the top of the cinder block wall. We could not understand why this could be because the construction contractor was reputable with national credentials.

We visited the mall with the contractor again within 1 week, and they could not explain the split. The split had now grown to 4 inches. We then realized the split was growing exponentially. We all became extremely concerned.

Upon reviewing his construction data, the contractor realized they did not perform soil boring prior to construction. They now learned the corner sinking was built on ash, a by-product of steel production. The land had been used as a dumping area for the by-product.

The solution to prevent further wall sinking was to pump concrete under the footer to stabilize the wall. Every 2 weeks, this pumping was performed for 1 year, all at the expense of the contractor.

# M

An elderly gentleman who owned an accounting firm contacted me. He indicated he owned a 36-unit apartment community, and the vacancies were increasing. He had owned this community for 28 years and was concerned and losing money. The community had always been successful with a waiting list at times. I indicated I would visit the community and get back to him.

Upon scheduling an appointment with the husband and wife management team, I then visited the community. They explained that they had been working with the owner for 22 years and admired him immensely. They had enjoyed an excellent working relationship with him.

Over time I visited the surrounding competition and noted all were with high occupancy. Then, I focused entirely on the owner's community, something had to be amiss.

Again, I met with the management couple for approximately 2 hours. In conversations I came to realize the neighborhood was changing, and this couple could not accept it. They were white and not comfortable with different colors of skin.

I reported my observation with the owner. He asked what my recommendations were, and I stated the only one was to replace the couple. He stated in a quiet tone, "Do what needs to be done."

After having interviewed several couples, one younger couple was selected. I inquired of the owner if he would advise the existing elderly couple of their termination. He stated again in a low tone that he preferred I do it.

We met in the couple's unit of twenty-two years, and I advised them of the pending management change. They indicated they saw it coming because of the low occupancy but did not understand exactly why.

The owner contacted me after a few months to thank me for everything. He further stated the new younger couple was increasing the occupancy and he was pleased. Within days, he sent me a thank you card with a $3,000 check.

Shortly after, his son, who was also an accountant, called and again thanked me upon behalf of his father. He stated his father just could not deal with the situation, in particular, the termination of the elderly couple of twenty-two years.

## M

We had foreclosed on an apartment community in South Carolina. The owner protested our foreclosure, and we went to trial. The community had been negligent for years with extensive repairs required.

With the testimony given for our company in the witness stand, the cross-examination became intense.

The owner's lawyer was asking compound questions of me, and we had differences when I attempted to separate the questions.

The whole trial was based upon the neglect of the community in maintenance. The crucial word was "down". It meant a unit was down because of maintenance neglect. This was the basis of our foreclosure and our right to do so. The community was not being leased because of the neglect, and we wanted to become the owners to prevent further deterioration.

The opposing lawyer wanted me to state that the word "down" within all our earlier foreclose documents meant "down," as in ground-level or first-level units. His questions of me implied this meaning, and more of his tricking questions attempted to do so.

After several back and forths with the question and my same responses, the judge stated, "I believe he (me) has sufficiently and consistently stated the understanding and as noted in the earlier document of the word "down" - please move on."

The jury agreed with our company position and allowed the foreclosure to proceed.

## M

Sitting in the office, I received a call from a contractor in Pennsylvania. He was requesting a $13,000 payment for work he had done on a stairway of our office building. At that dollar amount, I could not relate to authorizing the work, and the on-site manager was on vacation. I advised the contractor to allow me time to do the research.

After all was researched, we realized the $13,000 was a kickback. The company decided to prosecute this issue in Pennsylvania before a jury trial. The employee was found guilty and placed on probation. We could not imagine all other kickbacks potentially received, as one does not start as high as $13,000 with the first!

I also placed the blame upon myself. I thought I had the company's best managers at our properties and visited these the least because all went well. This was proven to be false, as other instances of "dishonesty" also occurred with the best and highly regarded company managers.

When opportunity allows, human weakness prevails.

## M

The apartment community was nestled in a forest of white birch trees. It was a federally subsidized community of 176 apartments within minutes of the beautiful Canadian/American border. One needed a pontoon plane to reach the destination.

Near the end of construction, actual construction costs exceeded the original project. Materials became the cause due to transportation to the remote site. We realized that our original rental structure would have to be revised.

We publicized in the local media the community's advertisement and the rents for the one—and two-bedroom apartments. The apartment announcements and rents were enthusiastically received, as there was a real need for such housing.

However, when the new rent structure became known, local citizens began to protest. The increase in rent was minimal compared to the original projections.

We worked in conjunction with the Federal Housing Authority and determined that a town meeting in a local gym was necessary to explain the reasons for the increase. All town people were to be invited.

After several meetings with the authority, we decided to have a morning meeting with me seated at an 8-foot table on the stage. The 3 housing authority dignitaries would be seated at a table up front with the audience. The authority would first ask questions of me, and after their questioning, the audience would be permitted to also ask questions of me.

The meeting began cordially; however, as the meeting progressed, the audience began to shout protesting comments and speak over the authorities. The authorities began to ask more damning questions of me somewhat siding with the audience. After halfway through the meeting, the authorities adjourned the meeting as their questions could not be heard against the comments from the uncivil audience.

It was unfortunate that the audience did not have the opportunity to hear all of the questions and my answers. Both had a legitimate story to tell. I knew all the questions and my responses before the meeting, as the authority and I had met and rehearsed both repeatedly.

The authorities had provided for me to leave under a police escort from the gym.

Upon construction completion, a management and leasing office was established, and occupancy was quickly obtained. As it should have, everything ended to the benefit of the community.

## M

The local HUD Housing Authority had contacted three local real estate personnel, including myself. Each of us represented a national real estate company with a portfolio of alternative forms of existing real estate throughout the United States.

Their interest was to inquire how we manage our apartment portfolio as private companies and from that how they may incorporate these policies and procedures into their organization.

We met 3 times in their offices, and each session was intense and lasted 8 hours.

The last session, although we scheduled 6, was the most intense with differences on 2 issues:

a) They indicated their rental collection policy was the worst and needed guidance to institute reforms. Within the private sector, a rigid policy is established within legal requirements per state for the eviction of delinquents.

This HUD office was within a state where the delinquent policy was precise, with a minimum turnaround time for the landlord to reclaim the unit from the delinquent tenants.

We distributed copies we obtained from our individual legal counsel and provided such to the HUD personnel. After their review and brief discussion, they indicated they could never institute our policies.

When inquired as to "why not," as such was an effective institution tool to manage apartment delinquent tenants. They quickly indicated many of the delinquent tenants were associated with the local government personnel, such as parents, uncles, aunts, friends, etc. They believed that enforcing such a policy would result in the termination of their employment. They based this on "words" from upper management as to the treatment of the "association of the government personnel."

b) They proudly provided a tour of their facilities. Upon viewing a room filled with approximately 60 large boxes, we inquired about their contents. They explained that all the computers were sent to them approximately 1 and 1/2 years ago. HUD's main office was to send personnel to instruct them to use it, but it had yet to do so. We offered, at our expense, our staff to assist with their use. They responded by indicating their home office would never permit the offer, but did thank us. The remaining three meetings were never scheduled or held. We tried with simple and proven remedies, but somehow, we failed.

## M

We projected a 3-5 year turnaround for an apartment community that we took possession of in South Carolina. It was in a nice section of the state, but the community was known for a heavy drug environment.

It consisted of 71 units of 1 and 2 bedroom units. We had a foreclosed legal proceeding for approximately 4 years as the current owner did not want to give up the property. He stated it was very profitable.

We quickly realized that of the 71 units, 69 were leased and we were impressed. However, as we continued with a profile of the occupancy we found most were single moms with children living with an abusive male companion.

After the arrest of a male live-in by the sheriff department, we learned the apartment community was known for being the center of severe drug activity. We met with the sheriff's department on several occasions and developed a program:

1. Seven sheriff deputies would be hired by our company.

2. All deputies would be given a free unit plus utilities for a term of 3 years.

3. We would not interfere with their approach in resolving the drug culture in the community.

4. They would provide us with a monthly report.

5. We would build an 8-foot chain-link fence on three sides of the community. At the top of the fence, black tar was to be applied heavily.

6. The deputies would be in uniform and armed.

The deputies would trade off on 24 hour shifts stopping all vehicles coming into the property. All vehicles meant those living in the units, relatives, guests, or others. All could be made to get out of the vehicle, padded down, and the vehicle searched.

Several arrests were made as a result of this.

At the end of one year, the occupancy went from 97% to 9%. Our home office began to panic but were kept informed on a monthly basis as to the progress. They also understood there were no alternatives.

The deputies were highly trained, professional, and pleasant in their demeanor.

Their shoulders were wider than railroad ties!

As soon as a unit vacated, we quickly repaired it through maintenance. After one year, we opened an on-site leasing/management office, and occupancy began to increase among young married couples and senior citizens.

At the end of three years, the occupancy was at 93%, and the community was respected.

The apartment community across the street then retained all of the deputies and implemented the same program, and the neighborhood began to recover.

We later learned that the live-in males would align themselves with single moms with children as a front to portray a family. However, they were the drug dealers of the neighborhood. They would financially support the mom and her children, and she would feel trapped,

The staff also reported often seeing a drug dealer running to jump over the fence by placing his shoes halfway into the fence while jumping. He would then grab the top of the fence and land on the opposite side. He then would start cursing loudly while wiping his hands onto his pants while looking at his tar-covered $300.00 athletic shoes.

**M**

As I walked into the entrance of a major department store in North Carolina, I observed 3 teenage girls. They approached a round rack of women's clothing. After selecting each, they removed 3 blouses and approached the cashier.

The cashier had also observed what I had seen. A defiant argument developed with shouting and finger-pointing. The cashier walked away and proceeded to a phone. After she had completed the call, she casually walked back to the 3 girls, smiling. After a brief conversation, the girls smiled back, thanked her, and walked out of the store with the clothing.

I approached this cashier and asked her, "What was that all about?" She stated the girls come to her story about every 4 months. They perform the same routine with the same story. The story is that their grandmother had bought the blouses for them because of a birthday, Christmas, or whatever holiday was near. "They do not like them" for whatever reason, which changes with each visit - wrong size, wrong color, do not fit, etc.

She is instructed to contact the company's legal departments to discuss each occurrence. With each occurrence, the legal department advises the cashier to just let them go. The cashier explained that the legal department is fearful of being sued should the cashier do something illegal while stopping the girls or saying something to them for their thievery. The stolen blouses would be less expensive than the company having to appear in court.

The cashier was upset because all was caught on camera and believed she would follow proper theft protocol. She is also judged at her year-end review on "shrinking inventory" in the store.

**M**

We were both young and a financially struggling company with children and spouses.

He contacted me for lunch, and all went well. I found him to be much like myself: ambitious, driven, and wanting to be successful. I was impressed with his rapid success when he told me the insurance company recommended that he obtain ransom insurance for his family.

Months later, on a Friday evening, he invited my spouse and me for dinner with him and his spouse. Again, all went well, but I realized it was more of an interview of me. His company was progressing rapidly and implied possible employment or a partnership, obviously, I was intrigued.

As we drove into his driveway that evening after dinner, he invited us into their home. It was late, and with a babysitter's time commitment, we had to refuse, of which we explained to them.

He had expressed interest in a professional organization at the dinner, of which I was the President. The following week, I attempted to contact him to provide information about the organization.

With no response, I attempted five to six times again and again with no response. I can only summarize that he was offended as we did not accept his offer to visit his home that evening after dinner.

The Monday after the Friday evening dinner, I had major surgery for a sciatic back nerve condition, which I had postponed repeatedly.

He went on to become highly financially successful and a millionaire. I went on to have a professional life. This book is a testimonial to this statement of life experience.

"Do not regret what you no longer have, but appreciate what you have now." -Maddie

www.ingramcontent.com/pod-product-compliance
Lightning Source LLC
Chambersburg PA
CBHW050606280326
41933CB00011B/1998